Christian Zen:
The Essential Teachings
of Jesus Christ

Christian Zen: The Essential Teachings of Jesus Christ

The Secret Sayings of Jesus
As Related in the Gospel of Thomas

COMPILED WITH COMMENTARIES BY
Robert Powell

NORTH ATLANTIC BOOKS
BERKELEY, CALIFORNIA

Published by
North Atlantic Books
P.O. Box 12327
Berkeley, California 94712

Cover and text design by Susan Quasha
Printed in the United States of America

Christian Zen: The Essential Teachings of Jesus Christ is sponsored by the Society for the Study of Native Arts and Sciences, a nonprofit educational corporation whose goals are to develop an educational and crosscultural perspective linking various scientific, social, and artistic fields; to nurture a holistic view of arts, sciences, humanities, and healing; and to publish and distribute literature on the relationship of mind, body, and nature.

Library of Congress Cataloging-in-Publication Data

Powell, Robert, 1918-
 Christian Zen : the essential teachings of Jesus Christ / by Robert Powell.
    p. cm.
 ISBN 1-55643-458-8 (pbk.)
 1. Jesus Christ—Teachings. 2. Gospel of Thomas (Coptic Gospel)—Criticism, interpretation, etc. 3. Zen Buddhism—Relations—Christianity. 4. Christianity and other religions—Zen Buddhism. I. Title.
 BS2415.P69 2003
 229′.8—dc22

                              2003017000

            1 2 3 4 5 6 7 DATA 07 06 05 04 03

≈Contents≈

Compiler's Preface

THE GOSPEL ACCORDING TO THOMAS comprises a collection of statements by Jesus to his half-brother, Thomas. There is a deep wisdom inherent in them, which gets lost at the level of scholarship. As implied by its subtitle, "The Secret Sayings of Jesus," the work represents an esoteric teaching, meant only for a certain elite. Many of the Sayings, if taken literally, do not make sense, and it is immediately obvious that on that level no meaning can be extracted from them. One senses that we need a revolutionary new approach to decode the scripture and make it intelligible, a situation that is commonly the case with esoteric material. The Apostles, with the possible exception of John, however, took the statements literally, and there appears therefore an entirely different Jesus before us in the New Testament. Properly understood, however—that is, with the proper magical key, we find in Jesus' Sayings a most beautiful presentation of the timeless teaching of *Advaita* (non-duality), the esoteric expression of the inner meaning of all the great religions.

Why do I use a term such as *advaita* which is so relatively obscure, at least in the West? No simple English word exists that approximates its meaning (literally "not-two"). The more familiar "non-dualism" and "non-duality" have been used to express the philosophy, but all these are only approximations as is even the word "philosophy." Perhaps the nearest Western term is "holistic," but even this does not cover it entirely. The point is that our ordinary thinking is strictly linear; ever based on pairs of opposites, such as high/low, good/bad, etc. But on the most fundamental level no such limiting parameters are recognized, since it is concerned only with the state prior to all such divisions. By the same token, it is essentially prior to all thought activities and categories. It expresses itself by a direct seeing, a non-intellectual comprehension, perhaps more akin to the appreciation of beauty in music or a work of art. To prevent misunderstanding, I hasten to add that *advaitins* do not deny the existence of good and evil but consider these as inherently and necessarily co-existent with the Universe, the mind, space-time. As stated so succinctly in the *Ashtavakra Gita:* "The universe is merely a mode of the mind; in reality it has no existence." Just as in a dream we are emoted by all kinds of things that upon awakening are seen to be products of a restless mind, so upon awakening to our real nature, we understand that our waking-state experiences are equally the products of a dream factory, and that in the Absolute none of these things really exists. Therefore, the only way of coming to terms with "evil" and participating in the Bliss that is our birthright—frequently referred to by Jesus as "the Kingdom of Heaven"—is through transcending the limitations of body, mind, and world.

How is this to be done? One may come to it if one can literally stay away from any purely intellectual approach to garner the truth. Man is so much given to "thinking" that any other approach in comprehening his life and his world has become almost "unthinkable" to him. I emphasize that the core of the teaching revolves around the question of man's identity, and that what is normally considered to be a person's identity is not his real self at all. The pseudo-identity is derived from an ever-shifting array of superficial sensory impressions from which one has constructed a multitude of images and concepts. Unless we come to terms with the latter, and thereby see the false as the false, the real will ever elude us. This, I believe, is Jesus' real message and teaching approach in these Sayings.

The Magical Key to Understanding
Jesus' Esoteric Legacy

THE CORE OF THE TEACHING and the essence of what Jesus Christ in himself represents revolve around the question of man's real identity, not merely his perceived identity. For what we normally consider a person's identity is not his real self at all. It is derived from an ever-shifting array of superficial sensory impressions from which one has constructed a multitude of thoughts, concepts, images, and associated emotions. To put the matter in a nutshell, our identity is based on the observation and existence of a particular body—the obvious product and evidence of the senses. This we take as the ultimate ground of our existence. The body is born and dies, and in the "in-between" lies our life representing the precious "me." Once this has been accepted, the first person singular, and subsequently the "you," the "we," and the "they,"—the entire world of persons and entities—spring into life. And then, simultaneously, there is the Universe, that possibly has its own life and death, and so on. This is the *Welt Anschauung* with which we have been brought up and have embraced so wholeheartedly and upon which in final analysis all philosophies and religions are based. There is only one thing wrong with this more or less pretty picture: *the senses themselves are suspect because they themselves, too, are the result of the senses.* For example, the eye that sees is itself seen by, what else?, the eye; in other words, the evidence is tainted—we are caught in a circular process! The seen is only evidence of a particular physiological process called "seeing." By the same token, that which is experienced as "sound" has no real, independent existence as such. The impression generated by the ear-nerve-brain complex is termed as "sound," but in actual fact has no real, independent existence as such; it is only evidence of a particular physiological process called "hearing." Similarly, for the other senses: In every case: the "observer" is the "observed." The great Indian sage, Sri Ramana Maharshi has illustrated this situation beautifully as that of the policeman who has caught the thief who is himself!

Thus, all things are necessarily reduced to an intangible "no-thingness," which is their ultimate and only Self-identity. This experiencing of the ultimate Emptiness of all relative things (their No-thingness) is at once the reaffirmation of one's absolute Being—birthless and deathless. Thus, when Ramana Maharshi was dying and his devotees grieved at the prospect of the master's imminent departure, he said: "I am not going away. Where could I go?" When such understanding is deeply and firmly sustained, it is often called "Self-realization," where the Self (spelled with a capital S) is indivisible and denotes one's real identity. And since it is not a concept, it cannot be described or defined; it can only be pointed to.

Scope of the Teaching

JESUS HIMSELF ADMONISHES that his teaching is not to be given to just anyone (see, especially, Sayings 62 and 93). However today, two thousand years later, there is a case to be made for lifting *advaita*, in all its expressions, from its esotericism to a teaching that is more generally accessible, naturally without proselytizing or watering it down in any way.

In this work I have presented the complete Sayings of Jesus (with the exception of about a dozen or so that were either unclear or for one reason or another did not seem to belong to this collection) in a form that should be easily accessible to all open-minded readers.

A correct understanding of the terminology employed in the Thomas Gospel is of vital importance in understanding Jesus. I am referring to one term in particular, frequently employed: the "Kingdom of the Father," or "The Father" in its abbreviated form, by which is meant simply the Truth, the Ultimate Reality, or the transcendental Self. In the other Gospels reference is made to the "Kingdom of Heaven." So when Christ declares: "the Kingdom of the Father is spread upon the earth and men do not see it," he emphasizes that the truth is ever available but men are blind to it. To appreciate how close this teaching is to that of *advaita* (in essence, they are identical), the great Indian sage, Sri Ramana Maharshi, stated: "The Kingdom of Heaven mentioned in the Bible and this world are not two different regions. 'The Kingdom is within you,' says the Bible. So it is. The realized being sees this as the Kingdom of Heaven, whereas the others see it as 'this world.' The difference lies only in the angle of vision."

Jesus sometimes refers to himself as "the Son of the Living One," which I take to mean he who lives by that very same truth of the Oneness of the real Self. Unfortunately, this as well as other variants such as "the Son of God" have been taken literally and thereby given Jesus a supernatural status that is not only unnecessary and unwarranted but will actually erect an artificial split in the consciousness.

Another significant expression Jesus uses is "Zone of Repose." In the context that he employs this term it can only mean what teachers of *advaita* refer to as "the area where nothing ever happens," prior to space-time or, in the words of Nisargadatta, another great Indian master, "prior to consciousness." It denotes one's ultimate nature—eternal, flawless, and changeless.

"To live in the Holy Ghost" points to the same verity indicated by the term "Zone of Repose." It is in line also with his paradoxical statement: "Blessed is he who was before he came into being" (Saying 19), emphasizing the timeless nature of man.

The Apostles and Their Interpretation

ONE PROBLEM THAT EVERYONE FACES who wishes to know what Jesus was really like and what he stood for is that we must rely entirely on the Gospels. In this connection the first and most significant thing that strikes us is the fact that Thomas speaks from an entirely different perspective than Matthew, Mark, and Luke. The latter interpret Jesus' sayings and actions largely from the dualistic level, which may or may not contain a core of spiritual truth, but the full impact in its absolute purity is received only when there is no interpretation by the intellect whatsoever. Only John at times seems close to grasping the esoteric meaning of the teaching. And, there are in fact those who hold that only the Secret Sayings of Jesus represent the true and original teachings of Christianity.

Jesus states very clearly that what his teaching is about is not to be experienced through the sense organs, or expressed mentally. In Jesus' own words: "I shall give you … what has never occurred to the human mind" (Saying 17). In this respect it is akin to Zen,* with its emphasis on direct seeing rather than endless cogitation. The inevitable conclusion and spiritual prescription that follow from all this is that our minds will never fathom the truth, and there is therefore a need to close down the mind, as it were, because whatever issues forth from the mental level is falsehood where it concerns the deepest matters. Worldly knowledge is ever based on memory and therefore belongs to the sphere of the past. This establishes a sharp demarcation line between ordinary worldly knowledge—with its subdivisions such as philosophy, psychology, science, etc.—and the spiritual, which is the area of the Self and is inexpressible in terms of words and concepts.

Another way of expressing this is: The Self is the Totality, and this cannot be defined in terms of its parts since that Totality is infinitely more than the sum total of its parts; it lies in a different dimension altogether. At the same time it means that the Self is

---

*The attainment of enlightenment by direct intuitive insight into a self-validating transcendent truth beyond all intellectual conceptions (Webster's Dictionary, 1994).

not accessible through any mental activity, through any *doing* on our part; such doing with an intent falls more properly within the field of psychology. What then is left us? There is only one way to reach the Kingdom: Direct seeing into and total comprehension of our Self-nature, our present imperfect state. Such immediate perception that completely bypasses the intellect has the capacity to dissolve the ego, which is the only hindrance to reaching our real nature: the Self that lies beyond space and time.

So long as there is no awakening to this situation one is identified with an "I," and there is psychological suffering. Self-realization is waking up from this dream of unreality, upon learning that there never was an individual "mind" or "self" in the first place. Only the Self, free from all divisions, and therefore transcending space and time, truly exists.

In this work I have presented the complete Sayings of Jesus (with the exception of about a dozen or so that were either unclear or for one reason or another did not seem to belong to this collection) in a form that should be easily digestible to all open-minded readers.

≈These are the secret sayings that
the living Jesus spoke and
Didymos Judas Thomas recorded.≈

≈1≈

*A*nd he said: "Whoever discovers the interpretation of these sayings will not experience death."

Those who understand Jesus' teachings will have transcended all dualities, including that of life and death.

≈ 2 ≈

*J*esus said: "Those who seek should not stop seeking until they find. When they find, they will be disturbed, they will marvel, and will reign over all."

Describes well the various stages of Self-realization. In the end, nothing will trouble the person, because he literally is the All to whom nothing is external.

*J*esus said: "If those who lead you say to you: 'See, the Kingdom is in Heaven,' then the birds of the heaven will precede you. If they say to you: 'It is in the sea,' then the fish will precede you. Rather, the Kingdom is within you as well as outside you."

In more prosaic language, Jesus might have said: Look, friends, you look in every direction, but always towards and in the external world, the world of space and time in which things apparently have their origin and where they interact. But in the spiritual sphere you will never find anything of value until you start looking within, and forget about events seemingly happening in the world. Once you start looking within and understand what you observe, you will transcend space and time and experience a reality in which nothing ever happens. You will understand that the Kingdom does not lie away from you but in fact is your very Self. Then the phrases "within you" and "outside you" will lose any meaning they might have had.

Self-knowledge is the first and only requirement; lacking that, one is really poor, in the true sense of the word.

*J*esus said: "The person old in days won't
hesitate to ask a little child seven days old
about the place of life, and that person will
live."

Many who have worldly experience do not
necessarily possess the innate wisdom of the
innocent. "Innocence" is something entirely
different from ignorance. It is a vital ingredient of
the spiritual life, the capacity to see things as they
really are, not according to some philosophy, an
arbitrary community standard, or a set of religious
tenets. It is the innocent one who truly lives.

≈5≈

*J*esus said: "Recognize what is within your sight, and that which is hidden from you will become plain to you. For there is nothing hidden which will not become manifest."

Just observe yourself and your actions and reactions in everyday life. After all, the spiritual life is the everyday life, and vice versa. Digest all your experiences fully so that they may not leave a residue and become psychological fetters. Then everything becomes clear to you.

⚈6⚈

*H*is disciples asked him: "Do you want us to fast? How should we pray? Should we give to charity? What diet should we observe?"

Jesus said: "Don't lie, and don't do what you hate, because all things are disclosed before heaven. After all, there is nothing hidden that will not be revealed, and there is nothing covered up that will remain undisclosed."

The disciples asked Jesus in detail how they should arrange their lives, as though Jesus could live these for them. Naturally, he does not oblige, just tells them to live a natural, straightforward life, to be honest with themselves and others, and to trust in their innate wisdom. In the course of such a life all the truly important things will be revealed.

≈8≈

*J*esus said: "The person is like a wise fisherman who cast his net into the sea and drew it up full of little fish. Among them the wise fisherman discovered a fine, large fish. He threw all the little fish back into the sea, and easily chose the large fish. Anyone here with two good ears had better listen!"

Jesus' message in this Saying runs parallel with that of Saying 76. One has to reject all the futile efforts by the mind to realize one's Self. Also: Discard all trivialities from your life so you may have time and energy to deal with the really important matters.

∼9∼

*J*esus said: "Look, the sower went out, took a handful [of seeds], and scattered [them]. Some fell on the road, and the birds came and gathered them. Others fell on rock, and they didn't take root in the soil and didn't produce heads of grain. Others fell on thorns, and they choked the seeds and worms ate them. And others fell on good soil, and it produced a good crop; it yielded sixty per measure and one hundred twenty per measure."

Jesus highlights the necessity for creating the required state of receptivity to enable absorption and maturation of the highest truths. *Advaita* can only flourish where the soil has been prepared and a state of readiness created. In this conection, see also Saying 93, which expresses much the same sentiment.

⇚10⇚

*J*esus said: "I have cast fire upon the world, and see, I am guarding it until it blazes."

An awakened man is bound to create enormous disturbance and turmoil in a world that is soundly asleep and whose values are directly opposed to true insight: wealth, security, psychological satisfaction, etc. But however much commotion such a one causes among the spiritually stagnant, he never desists, whatever the consequences in the world.

*T*he disciples said to Jesus: "We know that you are going to leave us. Who will be our leader?"

Jesus said to them: "No matter where you are, you are to go to James the Just, for whose sake heaven and earth came into being."

It appears from these Sayings that Jesus acknowledges only his brother James as having attained the sacred state of Self-realization and thus become qualified to continue the ministry.

*J*esus said to his disciples: "Compare me to something and tell me what I am like."

Simon Peter said to him: "You are like a just messenger."

Matthew said to him: "You are like a wise philosopher."

Thomas said to him: "Teacher, my mouth is utterly unable to say what you are like."

Jesus said: "I am not your teacher. Because you have drunk, you have become intoxicated from the bubbling stream that I have tended."

Our initial response when faced with something new is to compare it with something we are more familiar with. But such an approach will never lead to real understanding and insight. Again, of all the Apostles, Thomas is closest to the mark in relating to Jesus' challenge.

*J*esus said to them: "If you fast, you will give
rise to sin for yourselves; and if you pray, you
will be condemned; and if you give alms, you
will do harm to your spirits. When you go
into any land and walk about in the districts,
if they receive you, eat what they set before
you, and heal the sick among them. For what
goes into your mouth will not defile you, but
that which issues from your mouth—it is that
which will defile you."

Jesus admonishes his disciples that mental fasting is
much more important than physical fasting. More
generally, when faced with the general public, use
your discretion in advancing the teaching. Some
have seen this Saying as a further answer to the
questions raised in Saying 6.

≈15≈

*J*esus said, "When you see one who was not born of a woman, fall on your faces and worship him. That one is your Father."

This is the exact counterpart of Nisargadatta referring to a person as "the child of a barren woman." By the term "Father" Christ always refers to a person's real heritage, the Self or the worldless Reality.

*J*esus said, "Men think perhaps that it is peace which I have come to cast upon the world. They do not know that it is dissension that I have come to cast upon the earth: fire, sword, and war. For there will be five in a house: three will be against two, and two against three, the father against the son, and the son against the father. And they will stand alone."

As soon as the teaching becomes exoteric rather than remaining esoteric, people will become shocked and hostile, because they do not understand and are afraid of the unknown. They will defend that which they know but know not to be untrue, because this stance gives them a [false] sense of security.

*J*esus said: "I shall give you what no eye
has seen and what no ear has heard and
what no hand has touched and what never
occurred to the human mind."

This is one of the most powerful sayings of Jesus—
a clear reference to the transcendence of the main
senses of seeing, hearing, and touch, climaxed by
transcendence of the very mind itself. A beautiful
reference to the state of purity before sense
perception and mind origination exact their toll.

 *T*he disciples said to Jesus: "Tell us how our end will be."

Jesus said: "Have you discovered then the beginning that you look for the end? For where the beginning is, there will the end be. Blessed is he who will take his place in the beginning; he will know the end and will not experience death."

The end lies in the beginning. In modern terms one would say: "Learn first your beginner's Zen before looking for any end result." Then also you might really understand the meaning of what is termed "death."

*J*esus said: "Congratulations to the one who came into being before coming into being. If you become my disciples and pay attention to my sayings, these stones will serve you. For there are five trees in paradise for you; they do not change, summer or winter, and their leaves do not fall. Whoever knows them will not taste death."

Jesus here is referring to the Unborn, that which exists before birth and after death (see also Saying 15). The stones and the trees Jesus mentions symbolize the markers for the Unmanifest—prior to space and time—the realm where nothing ever happens and where death is not.

The disciples said to Jesus: "Tell us what the Kingdom of Heaven is like."

He said to them: "It is like a mustard seed, the smallest of all seeds. But when it falls on tilled soil, it produces a great plant and becomes a shelter for birds of the sky."

Enlightenment begins with the simple truth about ourselves—basically, the fact of our essential Nothingness—but ends with the truth about the entire world revealed.

*M*ary said to Jesus: "What are your disciples like?"

He said: "They are like little children living in a field that is not theirs. When the owners of the field come, they will say: 'Give us back our field.' They take off their clothes in front of them in order to give it back to them, and they return their field to them.

For this reason I say, if the owners of a house know that a thief is coming, they will be on guard before the thief arrives and will not let the thief break into their house [their domain] and steal their possessions.

As for you then, be on guard against the world. Prepare yourselves with great strength, so the robbers can't find a way to get to you, for the trouble you expect will come.

Let there be among you a person who understands.

When the crop ripens, he comes quickly carrying a sickle and harvests it. Anyone here with two good ears had better listen!"

Most people are totally alienated from their real nature, which is the Self. They are like little children playing with various toys of the world that enslave and blind them to their true nature ("steal their possessions"). Jesus exhorts his disciples always to be so open, so mindful, that should a rare moment of true insight arise, they will not miss an opportunity!

*J*esus saw infants being suckled. He said to his disciples: "These children being suckled are like those who enter the Kingdom."

The question is raised by Jesus: What is the role of knowledge in realization? A child naturally lives in a state of innocence. However, this state is not stabilized because with age his innocence disappears and he becomes knowledgeable, and with that knowledge emerges the possibility of corruption. Corruption occurs when pure knowledge creates an unreal center, the "I," and becomes I-centered and therefore susceptible to fear and desire. True innocence is a total lack of disturbance of the mind, a lack of knowledge that can be perverted. Thus, true innocence exists when knowledge remains stabilized; that is, when knowledge remains pure regardless of external circumstances. When all opposites have been transcended, and therefore all knowledge has been voided, and once again one is like a nursing baby full of innocence, then one qualifies to enter the Kingdom.

＝23＝

*J*esus said: " I shall choose you, one from a
thousand and two from ten thousand, and
they will stand as a single one."

Multiplicity into Unity: one, two, a thousand,
and two thousand—all these numbers are only
misapprehensions of what knows no divisions,
the One without Second.

*J*esus said: "There is a light within a person
of light, and it shines on the whole world.
If it does not shine, it is dark."

The light that Jesus talks about is no ordinary
physical light; he is referring to the Ultimate Light,
that of the Self, without which no other kind of
light could be observed.

≈25≈

*J*esus said: "Love your friends like your own soul, protect them like the pupil of your eye."

Not to do so would be a denial and betrayal of the truth of non-duality, for "friend" is no other than Oneself, and the very nature of the Self is Love. Jesus looked upon others not as different from himself, but as his very own self. We must meditate on who we are and gain the necessary Self-knowledge before we can help others on the spiritual path.

*J*esus said: "You see the sliver in your friend's eye, but you don't see the timber in your own eye. When you take the timber out of your own eye, then you will see well enough to remove the sliver from your friend's eye."

First, realize your own lack of vision or ignorance; then attend to the ignorance of others and the world.

*J*esus said, "If you do not fast from the world, you will not find the Father's kingdom."

This refers to mental fasting—disengaging oneself from the lures and attachments of the world—as a prerequisite for Self-realization. To be totally absorbed by worldly activities means you will be lost to the truth and waste your life.

≈28≈

*J*esus said: "I took my stand in the midst of the world, and in flesh I appeared to them. I found them all drunk, and I did not find any of them thirsty. My soul ached for the children of humanity, because they are blind in their hearts and do not see, for they came into the world empty, and they also seek to depart from the world empty. But meanwhile they are drunk. When they shake off their wine, then they will change their ways."

Most people in this world are intoxicated and victims of their senses, a situation they are totally unaware of. In other words, all are deep in *Maya!* Having absolutely no Self-awareness or Self-knowledge, they suffer. What is obviously needed is for them to shake off their intoxication, which can only happen through Self-awareness and Self-knowledge.

Jesus said: "If the flesh came into being because of spirit, it is a wonder. But if spirit came into being because of the body, it is a wonder of wonders. Indeed, I am amazed at how this great wealth has made its home in this poverty."

Jesus states: If the body has been produced by consciousness, it is remarkable. But it would be even more remarkable if the mind were the product of body or matter (as is still the thinking of many scientists today).

⟞31⟝

*J*esus said: "No prophet is accepted in his
own village; no physician heals those who
know him."

This expresses the well-known fact that familiarity
and the habit of seeing things in a particular way
often blind us to the truth about ourselves.

⟨32⟩

*J*esus said: "A city built on a high mountain and fortified cannot fail, nor can it be hidden."

Genuine spiritual insight cannot fail or be watered down; only half-truths can be diluted. Owing to its uniqueness it stands out in a world full of falsities and therefore cannot be hidden.

≈33≈

*J*esus said: "Preach from your housetops that which you will hear in your ears. For no one lights a lamp and puts it under a bushel, nor does he put it in a hidden place, but rather sets it on a lamp stand so that everyone who enters and leaves will see its light."

Once one has clearly seen the truth, be a light to the whole world. Have the courage to share it with others who still find themselves in the dark.

*J*esus said: "If a blind man leads a blind man, they will both fall into a pit."

This Saying characterizes our society very well. The world is full of false messengers making a lot of noise. The leaders as well as the led are equally ignorant, and so we have landed in this mess.

≈36≈

*J*esus said: "Do not fret from morning to evening and from evening until morning about what you will wear [about your food or about your clothing]."

Jesus reminds his disciples not to fret about trivialities, things concerning the body and its appurtenances—all this representing a complete waste of time and energy.

ᗞ37ᗡ

*H*is disciples said: "When will you become revealed to us and when shall we see you?"

Jesus said: "When you disrobe without being ashamed and take up your garments and place them under your feet like little children and tread on them, then will you see the Son of the Living One, and you will not be afraid."

The message here is: When you have ceased all concern with external appearances, which all relate to body-mind decoration, then you are open to That which never needs enhancement of any kind.

⊸38⊸

*J*esus said: "Often you have desired these
sayings that I am speaking to you, and you
have no one else from whom to hear them.
There will be days when you will seek me
and you will not find me."

Appreciate the rare occasions when you know
someone who will always tell you the real truth
about any situation, because he himself has no
vested interests in it. Such a one may be a realized
Master. Imbibe his teaching as much as you can, for
at the time you may need him most he may not be
there.

⤳39⤳

*J*esus said: "The Pharisees and the scribes have taken the keys of Knowledge and hidden them. They themselves have not entered, nor have they allowed to enter those who wish to. You, however, must be as wise as serpents and as innocent as doves."

Scholars on the whole have not been the best of guides towards realization; their keys of knowledge have not been of use to them and have actually put others off the search. So wise up by getting rid of all that useless knowledge you carry.

～40～

*J*esus said: "A grapevine has been planted
apart from the Father. Since it is not strong,
it will be pulled up by its root and perish."

Anything without a sound spiritual basis—i.e., not
established in truth—will not survive. "Apart from
the Father" signifies "away from the truth." Being a
falsity, it cannot survive the light of Truth; it will
carry the seeds of its own destruction. Therefore, no
worldly values can last.

*J*esus said: "Whoever has something in his hand will receive more, and whoever has nothing will be deprived of even the little he has."

The worldly person caught up in his possessions cannot help but accumulate further possessions; whereas the individual who has only disdain for material possessions will easily be detached from them, and those few possessions he holds are meaningless to him from an emotional point of view. But it also means that those who have the germ of a spiritual truth and cherish it will in time be spiritually enriched regardless of their material possessions.

◦42◦

*J*esus said: "Become passers-by."

This means: Do not have vested interests anywhere,
because these are properties of the ego, hallmarks of
limitation. Be totally empty, and live in the present
moment.

*H*is disciples said to him: "Who are You that You should say these things to us?"

Jesus answered: You don't understand who I am from what I say to you. Rather, you have become just like the Jews who either love the tree but hate its fruit or love the fruit but hate the tree."

Jesus points to the disciples' lack of understanding. They appear to have not the slightest inkling of what Jesus really stands for; they see him merely as a person but miss what he really is in a larger context, in his Source. Their understanding of causality is deficient in that they are the type of person who works towards a particular cause but then dislikes the result, or clings to a particular manifestation but is unaware of its cause.

≈44≈

*J*esus said: "Whoever blasphemes against
the Father will be forgiven, and whoever
blasphemes against the Son will be forgiven,
but whoever blasphemes against the Holy
Spirit will not be forgiven either on earth or
in heaven."

Jesus' Saying conveys: Do not worship me or God
but live in the Holy Ghost! On the individual level
you may not be in harmony with others, but when
you are not in harmony with your own innermost
self, watch out!

*J*esus said: "Grapes are not harvested from thorn trees, nor are figs gathered from thistles, for they yield no fruits. Good persons produce good from what they have stored; bad persons produce evil from the wickedness they have accumulated in their hearts, and say evil things. For from the overflow of the heart they produce evil."

Again, the message is: The inner ever produces the outer! Spirituality is mainly a matter of our innermost part, our very essence, being at peace with itself. Externally, this condition is manifested as beauty and bliss.

⁓46⁓

*J*esus said: "… whoever among you becomes a child will recognize the Father's kingdom."

Jesus reiterates the essential requirement for realization. A mature individual should attain psychological purity and be empty of worldly concerns (the germ of desires and fear), so that once again he "becomes a child."

*J*esus said: "It is impossible for a man to mount two horses or to stretch two bows. And it is impossible for a servant to serve two masters; otherwise he will honor the one and treat the other contemptuously. No man drinks old wine and immediately desires to drink new wine. And new wine is not put into an old wineskin, lest it bursts; nor is old wine put into a new wineskin, lest it spoil it. An old patch is not sewn onto a new garment, because a tear would result."

Dvaita and *advaita* are mutually exclusive! Do not mix things up and do not compromise. Once you have caught a glimpse of the truth, which is ever sparkling and ever fresh, be faithful to that true vision.

≈48≈

*J*esus said: "If two make peace with each other in this one house, they will say to the mountain, 'Move away,' and it will move away."

"If two make peace with each other in this one house" refers to the transcending of all dualities. Upon such transcendence of Duality, it will be possible to move mountains. According to the latter expression, it will be possible to do extraordinary things, but "mountain" here also stands for the multitude of things that ordinary worldly beings stand for, are identified with, and cling to. All that will have to be given up to make Realization possible.

≈49≈

*J*esus said: "Blessed are the solitary and elect, for you shall find the Kingdom; because you come from it, and you shall go there again."

Expresses the same sentiment as Saying 73. We can discover and return to the state (the Kingdom) before our so-called "birth" and after our so-called "death."

⮜50⮞

*J*esus said: "If they say to you, 'From where did you come?,' say to them 'We came from the Light, where the Light came into being of its own accord and established itself and became revealed in its image.' If they ask 'Who are you?,' you answer: 'We are his children and are the elect of the Living Father.'"

Ultimate Reality is often symbolized by the term "Light," from which the entire world springs. Objects and images have a source or underlying matrix, but the Light is Self-created ("came into being of its own accord"), or rather it is the Self and in Jesus' terminology is therefore equal to the "Living Father."

*H*is disciples said to him: "When will the repose of the dead come about and when will the new world come?"

He said to them: "What you look forward to has already come, but you do not recognize it."

Time is not, only the Present is, eternally! It is therefore useless to either look forward or backward; only the Now counts. The "repose of the dead" can be partaken of right now, while still in the body: "the world where nothing ever happens," in the words of the late *advaitic* sage, Sri Poonjaji.

⁓52⁓

*H*is disciples said to him: "Twenty-four prophets have spoken in Israel, and they all spoke of you."

He said to them: "You have disregarded the Living One who stands right before you and have spoken about the dead."

Jesus dismisses all this gossipy talk as unproductive, abstract and therefore dead knowledge. What has value is not hearsay but the presence of a living teacher who alone can effect direct transmission of the teaching and bring one nearer to realization.

∽53∽

*H*is disciples said to him: "Is circumcision beneficial or not?"

He said to them: "If it were beneficial, their father would beget them circumcised from their mother. Rather, the true circumcision in spirit has become completely profitable in every way."

This Saying holds meaning on two levels. Nature teaches us that there is nothing wrong with the uncircumcised state, which is our "given." If the circumcised state were superior, it would be our natural state. Secondly, we have not yet reached our natural state in the spiritual sense. The true circumcision is that of the transformation in spirit and is infinitely more important and beneficial than any physical change could be.

⁓54⁓

*J*esus said: "Blessed are the poor, for yours is the Kingdom of Heaven."

A true sage, even if he comes into some material possessions, cannot be bothered by them because he does not need them and is free from attachment.

⌘55⌘

*J*esus said: "Whoever does not hate his father and his mother cannot become a disciple to Me. And whoever does not hate his brothers and sisters and take up his cross in My way will not be worthy of Me."

See the great similarity with Saying 101 and its commentary, which is relevant here also.

⇒56⇐

*J*esus said: "Whoever has come to understand the world has found only a carcass, and whoever has discovered a carcass, of that person the world is not worthy."

The "World" is nothing more than a corpse; it is totally unreal. He who has found that out is not of the world: he is the Self.

⫍58⫎

*J*esus said: "Blessed is the man who has suffered and found life."

"Life" here means: "the cause of suffering" and the "transcendence of suffering." Simultaneously, he has found his Self.

*J*esus said: "Look to the living one as long as you live; otherwise you might die and then try to see the living one, and you will be unable to do so."

While in this body, take every opportunity to inquire into the real life—the life beyond space and time where nothing ever happens but where your Happiness lies.

~60~

*T*hey saw a Samaritan carrying a lamb on his way to Judea. Jesus said to his disciples: "Why does this man carry the lamb around?"

They said to him: "So that he may kill and eat it."

He said to them: "While it is alive, he will not eat it, but only when he has killed it and it has become a corpse."

They said to him: "He cannot do so otherwise."

He said to them: "You too, look for a place for yourself within the Repose, lest you become a corpse and be eaten."

We have already pointed to the fact that by "Repose," Jesus refers to the state of enlightenment—a place of absolute rest and bliss, well beyond the clutches of space and time. Jesus admonishes: Search for the Eternal or you will inevitably become a lost soul.

≈61≈

*J*esus said: "I am He who exists from the Undivided … if one is whole, one will be filled with light, but if one is divided, one will be filled with darkness."

Those who live in duality will never know the light of the Self.

⪧62⪦

*J*esus said: "I will disclose my mysteries to those who are worthy of my mysteries."

To understand and live in *advaita* requires a certain ripeness or maturity. Again, Jesus exhorts his followers to keep the teaching esoteric, and to share it only with those who are ready and eager for it.

≈63≈

*J*esus said: "There was a rich man who said,
'I shall put my money to use so that I may
sow, reap, plant, and fill my storehouse
with produce, with the result that I shall
lack nothing.' Such were his intentions, but
that same night he died. Let him who has
ears hear."

Doesn't this typify rather well how most people live in
our current society? He who banks on the process of
accumulation, both physically and psychologically,
ever living for the future, will miss in the spiritual life.
He will miss the beauty of the real, which is ever in the
timeless Now.

*J*esus said: "A man was having guests over for dinner. After he had prepared the dinner, he sent his servant to invite the guests. He went to the first one and said to him: 'My master invites you.'

The guest said: 'I have some claims against some merchants; they will come to me this evening. I must go and give them my orders. I ask to be excused from the dinner.'

The servant then went to another and said to him: 'My master has invited you.'

He answered him: 'I have just bought a house and have been requested to stay for the day. So I won't have time.'

The servant went to another and said to him: 'My master invites you.'

That man said: 'My friend is getting married and I am to prepare the dinner. I will not be able to attend. I pray to be excused from the dinner.'

The servant went to another and said to him: 'My master invites you.'

He said to him: 'I have bought a farm, and am on my way to collect the rent. I shall not be able to come. I pray to be excused.'

The servant returned and said to his master: 'Those whom you invited to the dinner have asked to be excused.'

The master said to his servant: 'Go outside in the streets and bring in anyone whom you may happen to meet so that they may dine. Businessmen and merchants will not enter the places of my Father.'"

The moral of all this, as pointed out by Jesus, is that the average worldly man has no time for and no real interest in a way of life other than the worldly one he has habituated himself to. The immediate satisfaction of the senses and continuing to live in the same rut are more important to him than the possibility of spiritual redemption.

≈67≈

*J*esus said: "Those who know all but are lacking in themselves are utterly lacking."

The key to the spiritual life is Self-knowledge. Without it, one can't even make a start, however much worldly knowledge one may possess.

≈69≈

*J*esus said: "Congratulations to those who go hungry, so the stomach of the one in want may be filled."

You must be really hungry for spiritual truths; then only will you receive true satisfaction.

≈70≈

*J*esus said: "If you bring forth what is within you, what you have will save you. If you do not have that within you, what you do not have will destroy you."

Only through Self-knowing can one come to Self-realization. Without that Self-knowledge you will unfailingly perish spiritually.

≈71≈

*J*esus said: "I will destroy this house, and no one will be able to rebuild it ... "

The "house" Jesus refers to is the dualistic structure of the prevalent worldview. Once the essential falsity of such a dualistic worldview is clearly seen, there is no foundation left upon which to rebuild it.

$\mathcal{A}$ man said to Him, "Tell my brothers to divide my father's possessions with me."

He said to him: "Oh man, who has made Me a divider?"

He turned to His disciples and said to them: "I am not a divider, am I?"

Jesus' audience would like him to be of the same cut as themselves, an expression of duality. Jesus, however, is not to turn away from his own emancipation and become a dualist or *dvaitin*.

⤳73⤝

*J*esus said: "The harvest is great but the laborers are few. Beseech the Lord, therefore, to send out laborers to the harvest."

Those who can harvest that which is precious and who have caught a glimpse of Reality are few in number.

*J*esus said: "Lord, there are many *around* the cistern [where baptisms are being performed] but nobody *within* the cistern."

Esoteric Christianity, as promulgated in these Sayings, is essentially world-renouncing. Therefore, Christianity in its purest form is not for the masses but only for the elect few. See the similarity with Saying 73.

*J*esus said: "Many are standing at the door,
but the solitary are the ones who will enter
the bridal chamber."

Only the "solitary," those who can go against the
majority view—the "chosen few"—will be able to
discover their real nature.

Jesus said: "The Kingdom of the Father is like a merchant who had a consignment of merchandise and who discovered a pearl. That merchant was shrewd. He sold the merchandise and bought the pearl alone for himself. You too, seek his unfailing and enduring treasure which no moth comes near to devour and no worm destroys."

Jesus clearly contrasts spiritual enrichment against worldly possessions.

≈77≈

*J*esus said: "It is I who am the All. From Me did the All come forth, and unto Me did the All extend. Split a piece of wood, and I am there. Lift up the stone, and you will find Me there."

This sounds like a piece of *Advaita Vedanta* literature. The real Self transcends all space-time limitations and is therefore incompatible with expressions such as "death" and "fear." There is nowhere that the Self is not present. That Oneness is the Ultimate, the essence of Life; hence the expression "the Living One" whereby Jesus designates himself.

≈78≈

*J*esus said: "Why did you come out into the
countryside? To see a reed shaken by the
wind? And to see a person dressed in soft
clothes, like your rulers and the powerful
ones? They are dressed in soft clothes, yet
cannot understand the truth."

Jesus reminds us that those so-called "great" people,
persons of wealth, of glamor, fame, and influence,
are not necessarily closer to the truth than the
simplest of souls. This makes the same point as
Saying 63, that people cannot be judged by mere
outer appearance.

≈79≈

 $\mathcal{A}$ woman from the crowd said to him:
"Blessed are the womb which bore You and
the breasts which nourished You."

He said to her: "Blessed are those who
have heard the word of the Father and have
truly kept it. For there will be days when
you will say: 'Blessed are the womb which
has not conceived and the breasts which
have not given milk.'"

Jesus seems to say: Procreation is acceptable, but
there is something much greater, which is becoming
one with the source of all creation, the Self.

~80~

*J*esus said: "Whoever has come to know the world has discovered the body, and whoever has discovered the body, of that one the world is not worthy."

This Saying and Saying 56 are almost identical, in which the body is equated with a corpse, and Jesus stamps him as a simpleton who takes the body for real. Naturally, he who has discovered the body for what it really is, a mere appearance in consciousness without any other tangible reality or finality, is superior to the world, because he is at once out of that world. He can view that world as only another object—interesting perhaps, but dangerously ensnaring if taken seriously (i.e., for real).

⪧81⪦

*J*esus said: "Let him who has grown rich be king, and let him who possesses power renounce it."

Let him who has (spiritual) riches and therefore real discernment be a leader of men, and the reverse: Let the ignorant man in a position of leadership resign so that he may do no further harm.

≈82≈

*J*esus said: "Whoever is near me is near the fire, and whoever is far from me is far from the Father's Kingdom."

Spiritual truths are like a fire that consumes one's entire worldly existence and its (false) values.

≈83≈

*J*esus said: "Images are manifest to man,
but the light in them remains concealed in
the image of the Father's light. He will
become manifest, but his image will remain
concealed by his light."

The "images" are the manifest objects perceived—
the realm of Objectivity—and "the Light which is
within them" is the Subjectivity. The Self, the
Unmanifest, remains unrealized so long as we
are held by the various sense objects.

*J*esus said: "When you see your likeness, you are happy. But when you see your images that came into being before you, which neither die nor become visible, how much will you have to bear?"

This apparently refers to the *samskaras* or *vasanas*, our innate tendencies that lie at the root of our present incarnation and thereby shape our being and fate. Indeed, we have all sorts of hang-ups regarding our physical manifestation since we are enslaved by our bodies, and these bodies are the means of gratification. But when it comes to our hidden *samskaras*, which have come down from our past and ever haunt us in the present, pity us for how much we have to endure!

≈86≈

*J*esus said: "The foxes have their holes and the birds have their nests, but the Son of Man has no place to lay his head and rest."

Those who follow and stay true to their spiritual destiny may have forfeited their physical security in society and the world.

≈87≈

*J*esus said: "Wretched is the body that is dependent upon a body, and how wretched is the soul that is dependent on these two."

This reiterates the insight expressed in a previous Saying, affirming that both body and mind are unreal and concluding that one must find the real Self, which is neither "body" or "mind." Only then one can be truly independent.

≈89≈

*J*esus said: "Why do you wash the outside
of the cup? Don't you understand that the
one who made the inside is also the one
who made the outside?"

Jesus admonishes us: Don't be so concerned with
outside appearances! First take care of your inner
being, then the outer (your relations with the
world) will take care of itself.

⮑90⮐

*J*esus said: "Come to me, for my yoke is easy and my lordship is mild, and you will find repose for yourselves."

The Saying hints in broad terms at the spiritual search, as pointed to by Jesus. The end result, that of "repose," has been mentioned by Jesus in other places, for example in Saying 60, where he equates the enlightened state with the repose of the dead. *Advaita* students will of course recognize it immediately as the place where nothing ever happens—the matrix of (i.e., prior to) space-time.

⁓91⁓

They said to him: "Tell us who you are so that we may believe in you."

He said to them: "You examine the face of heaven and earth, but you have not come to know the one who is in your presence, and you do not know how to examine the present moment."

Jesus castigates them for investigating all kinds of external objects—all in space and time ("the face of heaven and earth")—but neglecting to examine what is ever close at hand: the Self in whose presence one always is, in the precious moment of Now.

⁓92⁓

*J*esus said: "Seek and you will find. In the past, however, I did not tell you the things about which you asked me then. Now I am willing to reveal them, but you are not seeking them."

One must be really serious about Self-knowledge for spirituality to have any value at all. A guru or teacher can only do so much. Transfer of spiritual knowledge remains a rare and difficult process.

*J*esus said: "Don't give what is holy to
dogs, for they might throw it on the dung
heap. Do not throw pearls to swine, lest
they grind it to bits.

This gives the reason for keeping the teaching
esoteric.

*J*esus said, "He who seeks will find, and he who knocks will be let in."

Essentially, this states the same message as Saying 92: You are to make the first step in your search. But before anything can occur, spiritually speaking, there must be an inner urge for discovery and integration; otherwise nothing can happen.

*J*esus said: "If you have money, do not lend it at interest, but give it to one from whom you will not get it back."

True giving must have no expectation of a return.

⮜96⮞

*T*he disciples said to him: "Your brothers and your mother are standing outside."

He said to them: "Those here who do the will of My Father are My brothers and My mother. It is they who will enter the Kingdom of My Father."

Those who are related through blood lines are one thing; it is quite another thing to be spiritually related, to be real soul mates and share the same vision of life. For the latter are not merely related, they are One (the Self) and in Jesus' terminology "will enter the Kingdom."

⤙97⤚

*J*esus said: "The Kingdom of the Father is like a certain woman who was carrying a jar full of meal. While she was walking on a road, some distance from her home, the handle of the jar broke and the meal emptied out behind her. She did not realize it; she had noticed no accident. When she reached her house, she set the jar down and found it empty."

Most of us do not even realize that anything is wrong with our way of life, our clinging to duality with the attending misery. It takes some shocking event or great suffering to wake us up from our dreaming in unreality. The empty jar symbolizes the emptiness of our lives as currently lived.

Another interpretation of this Saying is its illustration that for a spiritual person nothing is ever gained or lost. The very idea of gain (or loss), of riches (or poverty), is to be voided, since it is based on ignorance of our real nature. Life continues—from moment to moment.

~98~

*J*esus said: "The Kingdom of the Father is like a certain man who wanted to kill a powerful man. In his own house he drew his sword and stuck it into the wall in order to find out whether his hand could carry through. Then he slew the powerful man."

To kill ignorance once and for all, much practice is needed and many efforts must be made. One must first get a feel for the obstacles to be overcome (testing oneself in spiritual practice) and then slay the dragon of ignorance (the powerful man) and merge with the Truth.

≈99≈

*T*he disciples said to him: "Your brothers
and your mother are standing outside." He
said to them: "Those here who do what my
Father wants are my brothers and my
mother. They are the ones who will enter
my Father's Kingdom."

Jesus points out that there is something stronger
than relationship through blood line. Those who
are one in their understanding of what *is* are the
true relations, because they are truly the Self, which
is One.

≈ 100 ≈

*T*hey showed Jesus a gold coin and said to him: "The Roman emperor's people demand taxes from us."

He said to them: "Give the emperor what belongs to the emperor, give God what belongs to God, and give me what is mine."

This can be summed up as follows: Be *in* the world but not *of* the world!

*J*esus said: "Whoever does not hate his father
and his mother as I do cannot become a
disciple to me. And whoever does not love
his father and his mother as I do cannot
become a disciple to me. For my mother
gave me falsehood, but my true Mother
gave me life."

The usual yardsticks based on the dualistic life-view
are no longer valid; that sort of love in relationships
has no validity since it is merely formal or mechanical,
and therefore based on falsehood. By the same
token he who does love another because of feeling
identity with his own Self—his true Mother—lives
the life of *advaita*.

∽102∾

*J*esus said: "Damn the Pharisees! They are
like a dog sleeping in the cattle manger:
the dog neither eats nor lets the cattle eat."

This should be read in conjunction with Saying 39,
where Jesus castigates scholars and intellectuals as
misleading earnest seekers of the Self. He admonishes:
If you can help it, have nothing to do with them or
their scholarly treatises.

∽103∽

*J*esus said: "Fortunate is the man who knows where the brigands will enter, so that he may get up, muster his domain, and arm himself before they invade."

Always be aware and prepared, so that the brigands of desire and fear will not sneak back in again and darken the light of one's understanding.

*T*hey said to Jesus: "Come, let us pray today, and let us fast."

Jesus said: "What sin have I committed or how have I been undone? Rather, when the groom leaves the bridal suite, then let people fast and pray."

Jesus hints that any spiritual practices are not to be undertaken casually or as a mere routine; they should become a natural and appropriate part of one's being.

≈105≈

*J*esus said, "He who knows the father and the mother will be called the child of a whore."

Here "the father and the mother" stand for knowledge of man's real ancestors, our spiritual origin. Outsiders will not understand you and call you by all sorts of demeaning epithets, merely because you are not on the same wavelength as they are.

∽106∽

*J*esus said: "When you make the two into one, you will become children of Adam, and when you say, 'Mountain move from here!,' it will move."

When you have realized true non-duality, there is nothing apart from you; whatever happens is experienced as taking place through your own Self.

≈108≈

*J*esus said, "He who will drink from my mouth will become like Me. I myself shall become he, and the things that are hidden will become revealed to him."

True understanding of what one is in reality, the Self, will destroy once and for all the vision of a universe peopled by separate beings. There will no longer be the "me" and the "you," only the He but that He is no longer a person.

⮾110⮾

*J*esus said: "Whoever finds the world and becomes rich, let him renounce the world."

The man of true insight, who has become successful in the world, will have no qualms in giving up all worldly gains, for he has seen through them and knows they are illusory. This signifies for him the end of all attachments.

≈ 111 ≈

*J*esus said: "The heavens and the earth will
roll up in your presence, and whoever is living
from the living one will not see death."
　　Does not Jesus say, "Whoever finds himself
is superior to the world?"

In that first sentence Jesus states that heaven and earth,
i.e., space-time, will collapse in one's Presence (that is,
in the Now). The message is very similar to that of
Saying 19 and is a clear reference to the transcendence
of the very mind itself. A beautiful pointer to the state of
purity before sense perception and mind origination
begin to extract their toll. The manifest world is to be
transcended, leading man to the deathless state.

⤙112⤚

*J*esus said: "Woe to the flesh that depends on the soul; woe to the soul that depends on the flesh."

This states much the same as in Saying 87. Matter as ensuing from mind or mind ensuing from matter—both are mistaken, since each has no independent reality. All this is merely a play of *Maya!*

⇜113⇝

*H*is disciples said to him: "When will the kingdom come?

Jesus said: "It will not come by expectation; it will not be said: 'Look, here! Or 'Look there!' Rather, the Father's kingdom is spread out upon the earth, but people do not see it."

The question asked cannot be answered in the ordinary way, for the kingdom is not at all a physical state; it is transcendental and therefore not limited in space-time. It has nothing to do with ordinary sense perception; it is Self-realization.

≈Glossary≈

Advaita (or "not-two"): Refers to the nature of what *is*, the Totality. This postulates: no divisions, and so no definitions. It therefore essentially negates its entry into a glossary such as this, which must be viewed solely as pro forma. Universally used to designate the final insight into the nature of what we are and ipso facto the world as observed by us. It is in the nature of things that anything expressed as a description or notation of reality is still itself necessarily dualistic, as otherwise nothing could be communicated. But there is one difference in this case: *Advaita* is the only concept inexorably pointing to its own destruction. Upon its full realization, it ceases to be concept. It destroys itself as concept as well as invalidating every other concept! Thus, the very notion of non-duality becomes redundant. In sum, Reality transcends the question of *advaita* versus *dvaita*, since this formulation itself is seen to be void. One is reminded of the very apt metaphor in Buddhist teaching: the thorn that is needed to remove all other thorns from the flesh and then, after it has performed this useful function, is itself destroyed. Such must be seen the role and meaning of *advaita*.

I take Christ's "Kingdom of the Father" to mean the same as the state of *advaita*, realization of the eternal Self, in which there are no longer any thoughts capable of disturbing the peace.

Advaitin: Individual who has realized the non-dual nature of Self.

Dvaita: Duality, differentiation, manifesting on the level of *Maya* or illusion.

Jnana: Knowledge or wisdom, seeing everything in absolute purity prior to the veiling of *Maya*.

Maya: Has been defined as "the cosmic illusion, more particularly the primordial illusion of identification with the body/mind; the manifest dynamic principle that projects the cosmic illusion and conceals the transcendental unity." It is probably the most difficult concept to realize, mainly because in actual fact it is not a concept at all. Most people have some notion of *Maya* as an error or inaccuracy in one's observation. Obvious examples are the rainbow and a mirage. What few people realize, however, is that *Maya* appertains to all observation, since in the most fundamental way any observation is flawed. The world perceived is, like a dream, fully unreal. *Ipso facto* what is real is immeasurable and inexpressible. An object of perception is ever a reflection of the perceptive mechanism itself rather than a separate reality apart from the percipient.

A profound statement occurs addressing this very topic in the *Gospel of Mary Magdalene*, which is also part of the Nag Hammadi Library that contains the Gospel of Thomas. It runs as follows:

> "All natures, all formed things, all creatures exist in and with one another and will again be resolved into their own roots, *because the nature of matter is dissolved into the roots of its nature alone. He who has ears to hear, let him hear.*" (Cf. Matthew 11:15, etc.)

Let us try to understand what *is*, for which we obviously have to start from the beginning (Saying 18). First, we need to acknowledge this world, which was there from the beginning of one's conscious being. And then there is a "me" located within that world. All that seems obvious enough.

Ah, but is it really that simple, is it really anything like that at all? What is the world, and what is the beginning? To use these terms, I must obviously have some understanding of space; and to talk about myself as an entity arising in this world, I must obviously have an understanding of time. Both arise with and through the emergence of body-mind, but other than that cannot be postulated or defined in any way. In other words, we have a circular argument, a self-defining statement; it is merely some noise by something that is still essentially unknown within itself as well as beyond itself. Hence, Mary Magdalene rightly states that the nature of anything or everything rests in the nature of its own roots alone. Thus, fundamentally there is no world at all, as we had envisaged it, and the "I" as an individual entity does not exist and has never existed. In other words, however strange all this may sound, there is neither birth nor death.

The Indian sage Sri Atmananda expressed the same truth in the following words: "Each sense organ perceives only itself, knowledge knows only knowledge…. A thing can prove the existence of nothing other than itself." This, in its broadest way, is the meaning of *Maya*.

There is, however, a further aspect of *Maya* that is equally fundamental, and perhaps even more so, towards understanding what we are in our true nature. The child, from the moment of his conception to shortly before or after birth, is nothing more than a physiological receptacle, collecting all kinds of physical impressions. His "mind" is a *tabula rasa*—or, which comes to the same thing, non-existent—and the receptacle's boundaries are purely physical, without as yet any recognition of these boundaries. All this activity takes place in a totally impersonal matrix. But it is not long before, through the magic of *Maya*, a psychological pain/pleasure center is born. The infant acquires an apparent persona or "self." And the non-dual state of Beingness turns into a "being" or "individual." At this precise point the "person" (Duality) is born. Yet, like a mirage, all of this is totally unreal, with the process going through all kinds of twists and turns to support the unreal entity called "I" or "me."